THE STUDENT'S ADJUSTMENT INVENTORY MANUAL: A COUNSELLOR'S PSYCHOLOGICAL WORKING GUIDE

MAUREEN EBANGA TANYI

(Associate professor PhD Educ. psychology)

Head of Department

Curriculum and Evaluation and educational Management

UNIVERSITY OF YAOUNDE, 1, FACULTY OF EDUCATION

YAOUNDE-REPUBLIC OF CAMEROON

Email: tanyi.maureen@yahoo.com

(00237) 675-810-935, 699-095-267

ISBN: 1534935509
ISBN-13: 9781534935501

Dedication

This work is dedicated to all those who have adjustment problems

Acknowledgements

The author is greatly indebted to the officers of the British Council and the Association of Commonwealth Universities who co-sponsored the standardisation of this manual.

I am also grateful to the following persons who assisted me to improve the quality of this work: Drs. Erick Parkins and Youngman, M.B., of the University of Nottingham, UK, I do appreciate the following Profs: Ohuche, R. O. (late), Nwana, O. C., Okpala, J., Nkachukuwu, Ama and Ali A. (Late), of the University of Nigeria, Nsukka whose initiative in the development of psychological instruments, measurement and evaluation spurt me to this work.

Above all, my special gratitude goes to Prof. Ako Teddy, the Rector of the University of Maroua for his administrative assistance in procuring the BC/ACWU award.

I owe much to my children, M. Tanyi, Charles, Ministry of Justice Yaounde, who translated this book from English to French, Justice Mbuagabaw, Peter. Bamenda,　Barrister Ayuk Confort Mbuagabaw Douala, Dr.(Mrs) Doreen

Mcgough, Manganese Paris, Justice (Mrs.) Patience Tanyi, high court Mamfe, misses Rose and Christy Tanyi - all were the source of my inspiration for obtaining the Senior Common wealth fellowship award that enabled me to standardise and cross-culturally tested this manual.

Preface

Three issues did come into play in my mind that spurt me into writing this Student Adjustment Inventory Manual (SAIM): One the lack of concern of the educators in Cameroon for those imparting basic moral behaviour. Two the increasing prevalent of immoral behaviour amongst school children and thirdly, and the most important is the non-availability of the counsellor's work tool or behavioural test. That is the lack of a behavioural instrument based on the socio-cultural background of the Cameroonian students that can be used to screen, diagnose, discriminate and measure the extent of children's behavioural problems with certainty.

This inventory is capable of identifying children behaviour in four different areas namely; personal, academic, social and emotional behaviours. Thus it is a personality inventory that counsellors should use to identify, measure the differentiate types of behaviours that children exhibit in schools from which therapy could be given. It also discriminates between adjusted and maladjusted children and even show the extent and area of students behaviour deficit.

The SAI is amongst the few psychological instruments (Like Bakere student's problem inventory) that have taken cognisance of the cultural back ground of African children because it has been constructed and validated in Nigeria and Cameroon and found to be worthy.

The SAI is able to discriminate between the behaviour of the European and the African and show the extent of each of their differences.

The Student's Adjustment Inventory Manual (SAIM) is the only African bilingual manual and the only psychological tool for Cameroonian educators. It can also be used for screening professional personnel like the military, medical, Judicial and teachers..etc.

SAIM content two sets of items and 2 systems of ratings; self and other –ratings to check the 'response set' of the rattee.

Contents

Chapter 1

Introduction

The concept of school adjustment

The term adjustment according to Shalfer (1936) in Arkoff (1968 p:3) is "a biological adaptation of the organism to it environment". The term adjustment according to this study relates directly to personality formation of an individual in his/her society. Personality also refers to stable variations in the techniques or process of adjustment. Stable forms of adjustment or adaptations can be regarded as traits of personality. Lazarus (1972) explains adjustment in terms of an individual struggle to get along or survive in his /her social and physical environment. School adjustment therefore, is a behavioural pattern that enables a student to get along with both academic and social demands of the school setting. Those that cannot meet or cope with the expected school demands or norms become maladjusted. This author then looks at this situation in four dimensions: personal academic, social and emotions. The extent to which

1

a child adjust or not in his/her environment is in respect to himself, others stimuli, his friends or academic activities. Maladjustment has meaning in terms of what a child fails to do and what he/she does that is not accepted in a given context.

The Student's Adjustment Inventory (SAI) represents the results of 17 years of intensive research by the author. SAI is a 57-item behavioural diagnostic inventory designed to identify, certify, discriminate and measure defective or poor behaviour exhibited by students in schools. It has been also tried on the university students and it proves positive. Psychologists and educators have long realised that many students perform poorly in their academic work not because they do not possess the mental ability to do well but because they do not adapt (adjust) to the school norms. This frequently leads to poor academic performance and ultimately, drop-out from school. To help curb this behaviour, the Student's adjustment inventory' was developed, standardised and cross- validated for application or used.

What is the student's adjustment inventory?

The student's adjustment inventory is a psychological test designed to identify, certify, and measure the area, extent, and level to which a child adheres to the school norms in regards to his/her, friends, and teachers in respect to the child's personal, academic, social, and emotional adjustment in school. It is made up of 57 psychological constructs and 57 statements that any psychologist, counsellor, and teacher can interpret in terms of a child's behaviour at school. They attempt to measure the area and the level of behaviour that is expected in school. It is used particularly for those who children have been identified as problem or maladjusted students from aged10-21 years and have lived at most a year in the school environment.

Chapter 2

Items Generation of Student's Adjustment Inventory

SAI Items were generated adopting both the logical and empirical approaches.

The logical approach

This author searched through various educational and psychological theories such as Freud, Alder, Bandura, Lazarus and Carl Rogers to generate constructs and elements that are correlates of personality and adjustment to produced items that appear to have relevance or relationship to all school behaviours. From this literature, 250 psychological constructs from which 250 behavioural statements were constructed. Through a rigorous validation exercises by experts in psychology, measurement of evaluation and counselling, that reduced the items to 72.

The empirical approach student's adjustment inventory

The empirical method involves the use of a criterion measure. A group of items that displays a trait to be measured is selected and its performance on that trait constructed with the performance of another group representing a contrasting point of reference. The items, which differentiate highly between the two groups, are included in the inventory. The criterion group which is made up of maladjusted students/ problem students were constituted using the Student Problem Inventory (SPI) of Bakare (1977). A contrasting point of reference was selected using the SAI. The 72 items obtained after the logical exercise was administered to the two groups of students, the adjusted and maladjusted (concurrent validation) the SPI inventory was used to test for the concurrent validity. Item editing, suitability and discrimination exercises were also done and this brought the items to 53.

The items that discriminated highly between the adjusted and maladjusted students were selected and were later subjected for another study "Cross-cultural validation of the inventory in England. The author took cognisance of ambiguity, irrelevance and cultural bias in understanding of the statements that are reflections of school norm behaviours that embodied the concept. In addition to the above exercise, an extensive review of literature in Europe during the cross-cultural study did increase the items to 57 adding 4 items to the inventory. The Personal Adjustment Sub-scale (PASS)had 2 items, Academic Adjustment Sub-scale (AASS) had 1 and Social Adjustment Sub-scale(SASS)1 item none for Emotional Adjustment Sub-scale (EASS). Again from the nature of the instrument and the sub-scales, it can be predicted that the items in each sub-scales may not necessarily be equal in number in each sub-scale.

It should be noted that the unequal numbers of items have not been consciously considered during item generation. The inventory was subjected to one pilot study and three field tests for norms of sex, age and socioeconomic status of the problem students and the validity and reliability as seen on page 12 were scrumptiously checked.

The 57- item of the SAI had 4 sub-scales of:

Personal   = 13 items

Academic = 18 items

Social   = 17 items

Emotional = 09 items

The items are considered to reflect maladjusted behaviour in both positive and negative direction. This is to check response set. The inventory is a 4-point Likert scale of

	Positive	Negative
Strongly agree	1	4
Agree	2	3
Disagree	3	2
Strongly disagree	4	1

The description of the sub-scales of student's adjustment inventory

Student's adjustment inventory has four unequal sub-scales that cover common behavioural trait from which diagnostic scores can be obtained.

A. Personal Adjustment Sub-Scale (PASS), it indicates the extent to which the student thinks about himself, his personal attitudes towards his/her physical or psychological environment, for example, "He is always untidy and or he does not always tell the truth". This items are coded as A1-13 items.

B. Academic Adjustment Sub-Scale (AASS), it attempts to measure the academic activities in school. In terms of finishing his/her assignment or attends school frequently. The code is B1-18 AASS that is it contains 18 items.

C. Social Adjustment Sub-Scale (SASS), this scale reflects the social activities the student portraits in relations to his friends, classmates and teachers for example, "Often say bad thing behind other students or getting involved in making fun". The code is C1-17 items.

D. Emotional Adjustment Sub-Scale (EASS), this is an assessment of the student's inner self. It is particularly valuably taken in connection with the other scores as an indication of how the child thinks about him/herself. The manifestation of his/her thoughts in relation to his/her outbursts in his/her behaviour exhibited in school, for example "feeling tense most of the time or daydreaming in class". This is the smallest scale with items that are not deliberately generated but fail to pass through the rigorous exercise of validation. It is the most difficult scale to identify It is coded D1 -9 items.

Chapter 3

The Aim of The Student's Adjustment Inventory

The aim of the student's adjustment inventory

(a) The inventory was developed to help identify students whose behaviour are defective and are bound to affect their academic performance.

(b) SAI will help the psychologists and the counsellors to improve on their services.

(c) SAI will aid the school staff to have a vivid and accurate description of the students' problems

(d) To help the teachers and counsellors to set a standard for close observation or assessment of student's behaviour.

(e) SAI facilitates behaviour identification and avoids wrong label and diagnosis.

The significance of SAI

Evidence has shown that most schools counsellors in even in the developed countries, Africa notably Cameroon relatively do not have a work tool of this nature that is self and other rated. Psychologists are no longer interested in instrumentation. (Car Rogers 1936 and Stott 1974). On the other hand, students are often inaccurately labelled by the teachers and giving wrongful names, (troublesome or stubbornness) where as the subject does not possess that time of behaviour. SAI could pigeon hole the various types of student's behaviours into their appropriate areas. This is why, it has 4 sub-scales namely: personal, academic, social and emotional adjustment. SAI does facilitate the work of the teacher, school staff and or the social worker.

The teachers and counsellors will be accurately informed on the type of behaviour and consequently the right therapy will be given to a student(s). It provides aid and the base for helping students to improve on their adjustment process.

SAI can be used on students in the upper primary school up to the university. But it is best when the subjects have had more than a year in a particular school environment. This is so because adjustment is a process that comes to play in everybody in a new environment. It becomes a problem if after a period of time the individual cannot cope with the various stimuli in that environment.

The uses of the student's adjustment inventory

Student's Adjustment Inventory is a teachers' /counsellors' rating scales. It selects with a fair degree of accuracy those children who are in need of therapy and of further counselling. It also indicates the areas of the problems within its four sub-scales. Clinically it is valuable with children who have specific problems since the scores obtained on the individual items will tell you the degree of the maladjustment of that particular trait, for example truancy, if strongly agree is ticked. This serves best to explain than hours of interview that a student may not conveniently give the right response because he knows it may affect him. Since it is other rated scale, the ratter may not turn to generalised results. This is why another scale the self-rated scaled is developed.

It must be noted that the SAI is not intended for use as academic test but it could be used as a behaviour assessment tool in either education or for promotion of workers in the industry since the items on the four sub-scales are based on personality development theories.

It also attains its best used when students are observed

for a reasonable period, say three to four weeks or records of the student's behaviour are obtained from the class teacher.

Student's adjustment iinventory as a survey or screening inventory

This inventory can be administered routinely to students towards the end of the second semester of the school year because this allows the school counselling services sufficient time to observe the subjects. It may also screen the students in case of special capability or efficiency such as "being independent or having initiative".

Student's adjustment inventory as a diagnostic inventory

The Student's Adjustment Inventory can also be used in identifying the sources of a student's academic problems and difficulties. Students who are not performing well as they suppose do relative to their mental ability may be suffering from defective behaviour problems. This may invariably affect their academic performance. The SAI provides a systematic and standardised way of identifying and measuring the level and area of problem in students.

Student's adjustment inventory as a descriptive objective tool

Student's Adjustment Inventory is a descriptive objective tool and is not subject to bias because it is not self-rated and the professional may need not know the subject before its administration since evidence of the victim's problem could be got from the school records. It also has a 'Student's Form' meant for students to assess themselves. The administrator has a wide range of choices of opinion from the four-point scales not "yes or "no" options.

Student's adjustment inventory as a teaching aid to the training of teachers

Curbing behaviour problems has been the most ardent problem that school psychologists and education staff are facing in some parts of the world including Cameroon. So the inclusion of SAI into the school curriculum would serve as a teaching aid for trainee counsellors and also as a motivating device that accelerates the transition from theory to practice. In teaching student teachers and counsellors how to identify and assess behaviour, the SAI can be used as a simple device for effective behaviour evaluation from which techniques of behaviour modification could be based and some major behaviour theories.

Student's adjustment Inventory as a Research tool

SAI has a number of research uses. It can be used to identify, certify, and measure the area and level of maladjustment in students through the application of the four sub-scales and the constructs underlining the items. For example, an item like "Usually takes things that do not belong to him", the underlying construct is, "pilfering". (See appendix 3 for the constructs).

SAI can monitor the effectiveness of counselling services. SAI will provide a reliable and valid measure of any improvement that may occur in the assessment and behaviour modification. The inventory could be included in research investigations for psychological counselling and educational processes, for example, the studies on personality are correlates of psychiatric variables such as delusions and or psychopathic behaviour can be seen on social and emotional sub-scales of SAI.

Chapter 4

Administration of The Student's Adjustment Inventory

The student's adjustment inventory can be used by a lay man because its administration is easy. Teachers, school counsellors and psychologists, some of whom may not be good in psychometric assessment, can use SAI. The instructions given to the administrator are simple. A brief description of school behaviour is written at the top of the inventory. This will enable the administrator (even a layman) to understand. The time limit is optional, depending on the administrator's discretion. The counsellor can decide to keep SAI as a 'behaviour cumulative folder' or a behaviour check list each time during his/her observation period when the subject exhibit undesirable behaviour, the counsellors checks the type of behaviour exhibited. There are no wrong or right answers like in the case of a cognitive test. If the administrator perform a careful observation at the identification stage, before rating, it is not surprising that the results would be exactly the behaviour that the child manifested.

Instruction for teachers/counsellors/ psychologists

There are 57 items describing the behaviour of students in school. Teachers/ counsellors/ psychologists are asked to identify students who show the behaviour that are described in each statement for each pupil/student.

The information obtained from this exercise is to be used solely for the purpose to which it is intended for. No data obtained will be used in any way to describe the ratter or rattee.

The instrument is use for different purposes: - to identify, to certify, discriminate and to measure the area and level or extent of the student's behaviours exhibited in school in four dimensions namely personal, academic, social and emotional. It contain a four-point scale of Strongly Agree (SA), Agree (A), Disagree (D), Disagree (D), and Strongly Disagree (SD).

You are expected to tick only one appropriate item that corresponds in each column. Even though the result reveals the students behavioural strength, it is important to indicate who has problems and who has not on each pupil's/student's inventory. Also give the B instrument to only those that you have been identified and rated by school staff.

Your students should be aged 10-25 years and must have spent at least 1 year in the school. It is most preferable to rate the pupils or students after two-three weeks observations in all areas of their behaviour- in class activities, play ground with friends, personal and emotional activities. Before administrating the inventory, it is advisable to consult pupil's /student's school records. The inventory may take 30-60 minutes to complete.

Personal data for each teacher /counsellor /psychologist (Ratter)

School_____

Class_____

Qualifications _____

Ratter's experience_____

Observation time_____

Personal data for each pupil/student identified

School _____

Class _____

Sex_____

Age_____

Scoring the student's adjustment inventory

SAI has 57 statements that describe behavioural activities that students exhibit in school in the four sub-scales. The items are both positively and negatively written and scored on a four-point scoring scale from strongly agree to strongly disagree. As mentioned in chapter one, SAI is designed to identify students with problems, those that score high on the scale are the maladjusted students. If the ratter ticks a positive statement for a positive answer the score will be lower than a positive statement for a negative answer and vice versa, for example, (see page 7 the scoring scale). "Always takes things that do not belong to him/her". If the ratter ticks agree (positive) on the scale, the score awarded will be 3 points but if the ratter ticks disagree (negative), the score will be 2. (See the appendices for the items and scoring form) The scoring for the whole SAI can be done in two ways:

(a) **Using a key**.

By using the 4-point scoring form with the letters abbreviated SA, A, D and SD representing the degree of responses. Start by assigning a positive or a negative sign to each statement on the left side of the answer sheet. Besides each item, use a ruler across to meet up to the column of the tick and then score the corresponding score using the scoring guide.

(b) **Using transparent stencil**

A transparent stencil can also be used with the abbreviated form of each scale (See p.7) and scores printed on. The administrator simply places the transparency exactly over the response area of the inventory and copy out the scores on each item and then later look up the corresponding constructs in the manual at the appendix 3. Add the total scores for all the four sub-scales. If the scores are **above** 2, it means the student is maladjusted and below 2 it means the reverse. It is advisable to rate all the items so as to obtain the full score for the inventory that will indicate the seriousness of the student's maladjustment. The score reflect the scale (4-point) and the number of items on each sub-scale is not reflecting the severity of the adjustment but the overall total score of the inventory except that the inventory is not completely used.

Some counsellors may decide to use only one sub-scale. In which case, the total items ticked will be subtracted from the total of the sub-scale. For example, The number of items for EASS =9 x4 =36. If the response tick is "agreed" positive for a Negative statement the score will be =3 if one happen to have such responses for all the 9 items. The score will read (9 x 3 = 27) (36 – 9) =27.

The tables of norms for the inventory can also be calculated by using those raw scores obtained from the subject's ratings for all the sub-scales and the total mean. The means indicate the level of maladjustment of the students at a glance. (See appendix 1, p 31).

Chapter 5

Validity of Student's Adjustment Inventory

Three studies (Excluding pilot study) have been conducted to investigate the validity of the SAI after the content validity was considered pertinent. To ensure that the inventory constituent provided the widest possible coverage, experts in instrument development rigorously went through the items. Different types of reliability and validity of the inventory was done to ensure SAI covers the subject matter, assess/measures the level and discriminates between a group of maladjusted and adjusted students.

The field application of the student's adjustment invent

SAI was developed and standardised in partial fulfilment of the author's doctorate in educational psychology in the University of Nigeria, Nsukka, and SAI was cross- validated by the author while on a fellowship award at the University of Nottingham, School of Education, Nottingham, UK. At this level, the scores of studies done on African students

(Cameroon) and that of the English (Nottingham/London) were statistically correlated and the correlation coefficients were high.

The studies are done first on 200 Nigeria students only, second on both 3,466 Anglophone and Francophone Cameroon students. 2,266 of them were identified maladjusted. Third study was with 213 English students, 147 were certified maladjusted and only 42 of them were used for construct validity. The fourth was a comparative cross-cultural study which was the most exhaustive study that has been made. Yet the validity and reliability were very high. This is to attest for the variability of the inventory given that the small sample size although the researcher has no apology to made. The sample identified were from the few schools that co-operated with the author.

Test 1: testing student's adjustment inventory reliability

The reliability of the test, this is the extent to which the test is consistent and the extent to which it correlates with itself. The test-retest procedure was done, that is administrating the inventory to the same group of students twice within the interval 3 to 6 weeks. The sample size was 200 students, (121 boys, 79 girls) aged, 114 old adolescence and 86 young adolescents The reliability obtained was 0.85 p. 0.05. The internal consistency coefficient obtained for the first study for the 4 sub-scales was 0.70, 0.40, 0.30 and 0.20. It is worthwhile to mention that the low coefficients are not surprising for a personality test on first application. More so, the items on the sub-scales measure different constructs. Each contributes to the entire test and so the procedure employed was to find out the suitability of items for the whole inventory and homogeneity of items within the sub-scales. However, the whole test had a co-efficient of 0.85.

Test 2: testing student's adjustment inventory reliability

The reliability of SAI. The aim of this is to ensure its stability and internal consistency. It was established through test-retest reliability using the Pearson Product Moment correlation and (Kunder Richardson). K-R 20 correlation was established for the sample size of. (N=2,266; 1,260 males, 1006 females; and 1,283 young and 983 old adolescents within a 3 week interval. The test- retest reliability was 0.88 p. 0.05 and the internal consistency correlation coefficient of the sub-scales was 0.72, p. 0.05.

Test 3: testing student's adjustment inventory reliability

The reliability found on this study through test-retest method using Pearson Product Moment correlation on (N = 41; males females; age: mean = 14 years. The correlation for whole test was 0.64* and that of the sub-scales were particularly high in all the four sub-scales, 0.91, 0.93, 0.90, and 0.86. It should be noted that the sample size for the pre- and post-test for the reliability of the individual items was very small. SAI still obtained a high significant level at 0.001.

Testing student's adjustment inventory validity

To see if the SAI measures what it is supposed to measure, SAI was validated at the extent to which it covers the content of the construct school adjustment by testing for constructs and concurrent validity. The content validity of the test was considered pertinent to ensure the instruments constituent items provided the widest possible coverage on the SAI and experts in instrument developments and psychologists did the validation.

Test 1: Testing student's adjustment inventory construct validity

Construct validity was used to validate the internal content of SAI for both maladjusted and adjusted students by using the t-test to find out whether there is any significant difference between the means of the two groups. The sample size used was (N =126 adolescents, 63 maladjusted and 63 adjusted) 56 males, 70 females, age mean 14 years. A t-test of 47.43 significance was obtained for the total SAI. This shows that SAI highly discriminated between maladjusted and adjusted students on a sample size of 63 on each group. The item suitability was done and the mean score obtained was 3.25 with a SD of 0.08.

Test 2: testing student's adjustment inventory construct validity

Construct validity of SAI as determined by t-test analysis of both maladjusted and adjusted on (N = 2,266, 1,259 males; 998 females and 1,195, 800 males and 395 females were identified as maladjusted and adjusted comprising the age of 670 young and 525 old adolescent students respectively. (3 missing items) The following means were obtained, total means 87.07 with SD of 4.64 and 39.31, SD of 5.81 for the two groups respectively.

Test 2: Testing student's adjustment inventory concurrent validity

Concurrent validity of SAI was obtained by administering a criterion test, the Student's Problem Inventory by Bakare (1977) that looks like SAI on the same subjects. A correlation coefficient of 0.91 was obtained.

Test 3: Testing student's adjustment inventory face and construct validity as a cross-cultural assessment tool

Experts went through the items for relevancy and did also consider cultural context of each item. Construct validity was determined by obtaining the mean scores of 2.60 with SD, 0.47 and 1.64 with SD of 0.31 from (N= 147, 100 males and 47 females maladjusted and (N = 66, males and females) adjusted students.

Test 3: Testing student's adjustment inventory concurrent validity

Concurrent validity was also done using the SAI Student rated Form. The identified students rated themselves and obtained a total mean of 2.34 with SD of .31. The correlation obtained from the sub-scales was as follows: .92, .62, .98, .93 and the whole test obtained a correlation of 0.83. Furthermore, scores from the problem students' ratting and that of the teachers' ratting were correlated and a high correlation coefficient of .98 was obtained for the whole test this confirms that the students were not wrongly identified.

Testing student's adjustment inventory norms

The norm for SAI was also obtained for all the 4 sub-scales, 0.57, 0.43, 0.96 and 0.69 with a corresponding F-Value of 0.33, 0.69, 0.00, and 0.10 respectively. The age (N = 86 young and 114 old adolescents were used to compute the Variance for all the 4 sub-scales and the correlation obtained were as follows; 0.01, 0.08, 0.10 and 0.40

Test 2: Testing student's adjustment inventory norms

Gender variable was also computed with 1,259 males and 998 females and the mean score obtained was 67.17 for males and 68.44 for females at a level of 0.00.significant.

Age 12-15 (1,218 young), and 15-+ (978) adolescents obtained mean scores 69.47 and 69.04 respectively at 0.00 level of significant.

Test 3: Testing for the norms

Gender 100 males and 43 females were sampled and the means scores were analysed, for both males and females 2.51 and 2.86 respectively at the significant level of 0.00

Testing for age the variable, only age 13-15 (62) were identified and the mean score obtained was 2.34 at the significant of 0. 00.

Test3: Cross-validation: testing student's adjustment inventory norms for both Cameroon and the English maladjusted and adjusted students

N=213 Cam. Students	Mean	SD	N=213 Eng. Students	Mean	SD	Sign.
Maladjusted	2.15	0.14	Maladjusted	2.64	0.31	p.<0.01
Adjusted	1.64	0.08	Adjusted	1.60	0.47	" "

The above results reveal that the Student's Adjustment Inventory is reliable, has a wider adaptability- could be used as cross-culturally to assess the level and identify the area of problem and thus it could be a work tool for behaviour therapists in these countries

References

Alder, A. (1972) Practice of individual psychology. New York: Harcourt Brace and World.

Arkoff, A. (1968). Adjustment and mental health. New York-USA: McCraw-Hill Inc.

Bakare, C. G. M. (1977). Student problem inventory manual. Ibadan-Nigeria: Psycho- educational research production.

Lazarus, N. (1976). Patterns of Adjustment (3rd Ed) Tokoyo-Japan:

Roger, C. (1961). Personal adjustment manual. New York: New York Press.

Stott, D. H. (1974). The social adjustment guide Manual. (5th Ed). London: Holder and Stoughton.

Youngmam, M. B. and Egglestone, J. F. (1979). Rediguide 10: Constructing test and scales. University of Nothingham: England: University of Nottingham Press.

Tanyi, M. E. (2002). "The student's adjustment inventory". *In Ife Psychologia*: *An International journal*. Ife-Nigeria: Ife Centre for Psychological Studies Vol. 10. (1) Pp.1-14.

Tanyi, E. M. (2007). The application of Maureen's student's adjustment inventory to the UK students as a cross-cultural inventory. In A. L. Comnuian, and R. Roth, (Eds.). *International perspective in psychology*. Germany Aachen: Shaker Verlag Pp107-121.

Appendix 1

The student's adjustment inventory

School experience shows that students who are well adjusted in school show more interest in their academic pursuits by completing class and home work. They do go to school on time and frequently. They tend to dress neatly and cooperate with other peers and teachers. They also accept school rules and regulations, exhibit high self-esteem and have a good emotional state. This is not the case with some other students, who are said to have problems in school.

Instructions for teachers/counsellors/ psychologists

There are 57 items describing the behaviour of students in school. Teachers/ counsellors/ psychologists are asked to identify students who manifest the behaviour that are described in each statement for each pupil/student below.

Your students should be aged 10-25 and must have spent at least 1 year in that school environment. It is most preferable to rate the pupils or students after three- 6 weeks observations in all areas of their behaviours. You can apply the whole test - in class activities, a playground with friends, personal and emotional activities. But if you want to apply only one sub-scale you can then observe the child for that sub-scale. It is advisable to consult pupils /student's school records. The inventory will take 30-60 minutes to complete.

The instrument is use for different purposes: - to identify, to certify, discriminate and to measure the area and level of the student's behaviours exhibited in school in four dimensions. It is important to indicate who has problems and who has not on each pupil/ student's questionnaire even though the result will indicate. The instrument is also other ratted that is, the students can rate themselves. This will help the ratter to calculate concurrent validity.

It is only the statements that are given out to students or whoever is rating. The construct are kept by the tatters/teachers for eventual use to identify the type of behaviour that the student exhibits.

This inventory covers four dimensions of school behaviours and uses a four-point scale of;

Strongly Agree (SA), Agree (A), Disagree (D), Disagree (D), Strongly Disagree (SD).

Please tick the appropriate column.

Personal data for each teacher /school counsellor/psychologist to be used for each child (Ratter's form)

School _____

Class_____

Sex _____

Qualifications _____

Ratter's experience_____

N	Do not write in this column	Statement: Scale A Personal adjustment 13 items	SA	A	D	SD
1		Does not often tell the truth.	4	3	2	1
2		Prefers to be idle	4	3	2	1
3		Often looks untidy	4	3	2	1
4		Finds it difficult to speak in the classroom when asked to speak.	4	3	2	1
5		Often fights with peers.	4	3	2	1
6		Usually stays alone	4	3	2	1
7		Regularly forgets	4	3	2	1
8		Often takes things that do not belong to him/her.	4	3	2	1
9		Always annoyed over minor issues	4	3	2	1
10		Always obey class rules (reversed)	1	2	3	4
11		Often gets involved in school punishment	4	3	2	1
12		Usually takes decisions even if others disagree (reversed)	1	2	3	4

13		Does often argue what friends say	4	3	2	1
		Scale B: Academic adjustment 18 items				
14		Does not attend school frequently	4	3	2	1
15		Tends to do what is expected without having to be told	4	3	2	1
16		Does not like sharing even ideas in class.	4	3	2	1
17		Always seeks academic help from peers and teachers (reversed)	1	2	3	4
18		Does not appear to be worried when obtained low scores in a test	4	3	2	1
19		Often cheats in tests and examinations	4	3	2	1
20		Does not like finishing his/her assignments	4	3	2	1
21		Often brings new ideas during class discussions (reversed)	1	2	3	4
22		Does not take risks at all	4	3	2	1
23		Does not like to do extra class work	4	3	2	1
24		Often imaginative (reversed)	1	2	3	4
25		keeps long hours at work without distraction	4	3	2	1
26		Makes no effort to understand lessons	4	3	2	1
27		Often misplacing school books	4	3	2	1
28		Wants to answer questions but never gets them right.	4	3	2	1
29		Often fidgets in class	4	3	2	1
30		Feels more intelligent than others (reversed)	1	2	3	4
31		Complains of too much work in school	4	3	2	1
		Scale C. Social adjustment 17 items				
32		Likes shouting at junior peers	4	3	2	1

33		Unable to lead other students	4	3	2	1
34		Cannot stand a large crowd	4	3	2	1
35		Often picks on other students	4	3	2	1
36		Always relays on what friends say	4	3	2	1
37		Does not exercise his/her rights	4	3	2	1
38		Always say bad things about other students	4	3	2	1
39		Has 'I don't care' attitudes	4	3	2	1
40		Never likes mixing with the opposite sex	4	3	2	1
41		Likes mixing-up with others (reversed)	1	2	3	4
42		Usually threatens to fight other peers	4	3	2	1
43		Tends to insult others a lot	4	3	2	1
44		Not interested in finding out new ideas	4	3	2	1
45		Never keeps friends for long	4	3	2	1
46		Not willing to work with the leader of the group	4	3	2	1
47		Usually uses bad language even to the teachers	4	3	2	1
48		Often gets involved in making fun	4	3	2	1
		Scale D: Emotional adjustment 9 items				
49		Feels tense most of the time	4	3	2	1
50		Looks happy in class (reversed)	1	2	3	4
51		Often seems not relax in class	4	3	2	1
52		Makes a lot of noise in class	4	3	2	1
53		Often daydreams	4	3	2	1
54		Sometimes talks alone	4	3	2	1
55		Usually feels tired or lacks energy	4	3	2	1
56		Often looses temper for no reason	4	3	2	1
57		Jokes a lot with friends (reversed)	1	2	3	4

Appendix 2

Student's Adjustment Inventory (student's form)

Pupils/ student's self-rating scale

Personal data for each pupil/student identified with problems:

Name_____

School_____

Class_____

Sex_____

Age_____

Parents' occupation_____

Parents' civil status_____

This inventory covers four dimensions of school behaviours and uses a four-point scale of;

Strongly Agree (SA), Agree (A), Disagree (D), Disagree (D), Strongly Disagree (SD).

Please tick the appropriate column.

How to score the **ADJUSTMENT INVENTORY** scales.

(See manual Chapter 4, pages 15-20 for instructions)

N	Do not write in this column	Statement: Scale A Personal Adjustment 13 items	SA	A	D	SD
1		My teachers always punish me to speak the truth.	4	3	2	1
2		Our teacher always gives us too much work to do	4	3	2	1
3		Often looks untidy	4	3	2	1
4		It is difficult to speak in the classroom when asked to speak.	4	3	2	1
5		Peers often fight me.	4	3	2	1
6		Friends always worry me	4	3	2	1
7		I do not bother much remembering things	4	3	2	1
8		Do friends often accuse you of talking their things	4	3	2	1
9		Many issues always annoyed in school	4	3	2	1
10		Teachers often imposes laws on me/us (reversed)	1	2	3	4
11		My teacher hates me that is why she/he always punishes me	4	3	2	1
12		Friends usually forced me to accept what think (reversed)	1	2	3	4
13		I do agree with friends and teachers on all issues raised	4	3	2	1
		Scale B: Academic Adjustment 18 items				
14		Our school is boring	4	3	2	1
15		I know what to do whenever I have a problem	4	3	2	1
16		Friends do not like	4	3	2	1

		sharing even ideas in class with me.				
17		My best friends usually help me with my work (reversed)	1	2	3	4
18		Our teacher is fun of giving difficult tests	4	3	2	1
19		Our teacher often accused me of cheating in tests and examinations	4	3	2	1
20		There is so much to do that I hardly finish my assignments	4	3	2	1
21		Friends always want me to be involve in some issues that are not important (reversed)	1	2	3	4
22		Involving in many class activities is risky	4	3	2	1
23		Our teacher likes giving us too much assignments /class work	4	3	2	1
24		Thinking of things to do is sometimes very boring (reversed)	1	2	3	4
25		Our lecture hours are usually quite long and so causes distraction	4	3	2	1
26		Our teacher do not explain things well for me to understand	4	3	2	1
27		Friends have stolen all my books	4	3	2	1
28		I do always answer questions but teacher never ticks them right.	4	3	2	1
29		I like explaining things to fiends but the teacher will always shout at me in class	4	3	2	1
30		Our class is in a mess because friends do not	1	2	3	4

			4	3	2	1
		reason as I do (reversed)				
31		School activities are not interesting	4	3	2	1
		Scale C. Social Adjustment 17 items				
32		I do not expect junior peers or students to talk to me	4	3	2	1
33		Friends always forced me to be at the forefront	4	3	2	1
34		Large crowd discourages one to talk	4	3	2	1
35		Friends often pick on me for no reason	4	3	2	1
36		Ideas from friends are usually very important	4	3	2	1
37		Opinions from friends are always rights and better	4	3	2	1
38		Friends always tell me bad things about other students	4	3	2	1
39		'I don't care', I do live my life the way I want to	4	3	2	1
40		Girls like to disturb us a lot	4	3	2	1
41		I usually like mixing-up with others (reversed	1	2	3	4
42		Friends usually threatens to fight me	4	3	2	1
43		Friends always insult me for nothing	4	3	2	1
44		I do not like getting involve on things that do not concern me	4	3	2	1
45		Friends usually disturbed my peace	4	3	2	1
46		Our delegate/leader is not compromising with us	4	3	2	1
47		They always accused me for insulting them	4	3	2	1
48		Making fun is usually dangerous	4	3	2	1

		Scale D: Emotional Adjustment 9 items				
49		It is always good to think of pass issues	4	3	2	1
50		I am not usually happy in class (reversed)	1	2	3	4
51		I feel sometimes not relax in class	4	3	2	1
52		I feel good when we have class debate or discussions	4	3	2	1
53		I like to be left alone	4	3	2	1
54		Sometimes is best to think deeply	4	3	2	1
55		I usually feels tired or lacks energy	4	3	2	1
56		Most of the time friends say things that annoys me	4	3	2	1
57		I loved joking a lot with friends (reversed)	1	2	3	4

This is the KEY to determine exactly the time of behaviour students are exhibiting in schools. Each statement describes a construct as seen below. It is easier to use a stencil for a vivid assessment

Behaviour identification through items

N	Behaviour quality	Statement: Scale A 13 items	SA	A	D	SD
1	Liar	Does not often tell the truth.	4	3	2	1
2	Laziness	Prefers to be idle	4	3	2	1
3	Tidiness	Often looks untidy	4	3	2	1
4	Shyness	Finds it difficult to speak in the classroom when asked to speak.	4	3	2	1
5	Violence	Often fights with peers.	4	3	2	1
6	Isolate	Usually stays alone	4	3	2	1
7	Forgetfulnes s	Regularly forgets	4	3	2	1
8	Pilfering	Often takes things that do not belong to him/her.	4	3	2	1
9	Quick temper	Always annoyed over minor issues	4	3	2	1
10	Obedience	Always obey the rules in class (reversed)	1	2	3	4
11	Stubbornnes s	Often gets involved in school punishment	4	3	2	1
12	Firmness	Usually takes decisions even if others disagree (reversed)	1	2	3	4
13	Submissiven	Does not often accept what friends	4	3	2	1

	ess	say without arguing				
		Scale B: Academic Adjustment 18 items				
14	Truancy	Does not attend school frequently	4	3	2	1
15	Responsibilit y	Tends to do what is expected without having to be told	4	3	2	1
16	Egoistic	Does not like sharing even ideas in class.	4	3	2	1
17	Dependency	Always seeks academic help from peers and teacher (reversed)	1	2	3	4
18	Ambitious	Does not appear to be worried when obtained low scores in a test	4	3	2	1
19	Fraudulent	Often cheats in tests and examinations	4	3	2	1
20	Determinati on	Does not like finishing his/her assignments	4	3	2	1
21	Initiative	Always brings new ideas during class discussions (reversed)	1	2	3	4
22	Adventurous	Does not take risks at all	4	3	2	1
23	Hardworkin g	Does not like to do extra class work	4	3	2	1
24	Creativity	Often imaginative (reversed)	1	2	3	4
25	Concentratio n	keeps long hours at work without distraction	4	3	2	1
26	Diligence	Makes no effort to understand lessons	4	3	2	1
27	Carelessness	Often misplacing school books	4	3	2	1
28	Competence	Wants to answer questions but never gets them right.	4	3	2	1
29	Excitability	Often fidgets in class	4	3	2	1
30	Self-esteem	Feels more intelligent than others (reversed)	1	2	3	4
31	School phobia	Complains of too much work in school	4	3	2	1
		Scale C. Social Adjustment 17 items				

32	Bully	Likes shouting at junior peers or students	4	3	2	1
33	Leadership	Unable to lead other students	4	3	2	1
34	Introvert	Cannot stand a large crowd	4	3	2	1
35	Abuse	Often picks on other students	4	3	2	1
36	Confidence	Always relays on what friends say	4	3	2	1
37	Assertive	Does not exercise his/her rights in a situation	4	3	2	1
38	Gossip	Always say bad things about other students.	4	3	2	1
39	Irresponsible	Has 'I don't care' attitudes	4	3	2	1
40	Sex phobia	Never likes mixing with the opposite sex	4	3	2	1
41	Social interaction	Likes sharing ideas in the group (reversed)	1	2	3	4
42	Aggressiveness	Usually threatens to fight other peers	4	3	2	1
43	Quarrelsome	Tends to insult others a lot	4	3	2	1
44	Inquisitive	Not interested in finding out new ideas	4	3	2	1
45	Unfriendly	Never keeps friends for long	4	3	2	1
46	Uncooperative	Not willing to work with the leader of the group	4	3	2	1
47	Sullen	Usually uses bad language even to the teacher	4	3	2	1
48	Jovial	Often gets involved in making fun	4	3	2	1
		Scale D: Emotional Adjustment 9 items				
49	Moody	Feels tense most of the time	4	3	2	1
50	Happiness	Looks happy in class (reversed)	1	2	3	4
51	Restlessness	Often seems uneasy in class	4	3	2	1
52	Hyper-active	Makes a lot of noise in class	4	3	2	1
53	Withdrawn	Often daydreams	4	3	2	1
54	Stressful	Sometimes talks alone	4	3	2	1
55	Weakness	Usually feels tired or lacks energy	4	3	2	1
56	Temperament	Often looses temper for no reason	4	3	2	1

| 57 | Playful | Jokes a lot with friends (reversed) | 1 | 2 | 3 | 4 |

Appendix 4

Student's Adjustment Inventory Self-Rating (Student's Form)

Personal Adjustment

N	Behaviour Quality	Statement: Scale A 13 items	SA	A	D	SD
1	Liar	My teachers always ask me to speak the truth.	4	3	2	1
2	Laziness	Our teacher always gives us too much work to do	4	3	2	1
3	Tidiness	Often looks untidy	4	3	2	1
4	Shyness	It is difficult to speak in the classroom when asked to speak.	4	3	2	1
5	Violence	Peers often fight me.	4	3	2	1
6	Isolate	Friends always worry me	4	3	2	1
7	Forgetfulness	I do not bother much remember things	4	3	2	1
8	Pilfering	Do friends often accuse you of talking their things	4	3	2	1
9	Quick temper	Many issues always annoyed in school	4	3	2	1
10	Obedience	Teachers often imposes things on me/us to do (reversed)	1	2	3	4
11	Stubbornness	My teacher hates me that is why she/he always punishes me	4	3	2	1
12	Firmness	Friends usually forced me to accept what think (reversed)	1	2	3	4
13	Submissiveness	I do agree with friends and teachers on all issues raised	4	3	2	1

		Scale B: Academic Adjustment 18 items				
14	Truancy	Our school is boring	4	3	2	1
15	Responsibility	I know what to do whenever I have a problem	4	3	2	1
16	Egoistic	Friends do not like sharing even ideas in class with me.	4	3	2	1
17	Dependency	My best Friends usually help me with my work (reversed)	1	2	3	4
18	Ambitious	Our teacher id fun of giving difficult test	4	3	2	1
19	Fraudulent	Our teacher often accused me of cheating in tests and examinations	4	3	2	1
20	Determination	There is so much to do that I hardly finish my assignments	4	3	2	1
21	Initiative	I do not always bore myself so much strange class discussions (reversed)	1	2	3	4
22	Adventurous	Involving in many class activities is risky	4	3	2	1
23	Hardworking	Our teacher likes giving us too much assignments class work	4	3	2	1
24	Creativity	Thinking of things to do is often boring (reversed)	1	2	3	4
25	Concentration	Our lecture hours are usually quite long and so causes distraction	4	3	2	1
26	Diligence	Our teacher do not explain things well for me to understand lessons	4	3	2	1
27	Carelessness	Friends have stolen all my books	4	3	2	1
28	Competence	I do always answer questions but teacher never ticks them right.	4	3	2	1
29	Excitability	I like explaining things to fiends but the teacher will always shout	4	3	2	1

		at me in class				
30	Self-esteem	Our class is in a mess because friends do not reason as I do (reversed)	1	2	3	4
31	School phobia	School activities are not interesting	4	3	2	1
		Scale C. Social Adjustment 17 items				
32	Bully	I do not expect junior peers or students to talk to me	4	3	2	1
33	Leadership	Friends always want me to be at the forefront	4	3	2	1
34	Introvert	Large crowd discourages one to talk	4	3	2	1
35	Abuse	Friends often pick on me for no reason	4	3	2	1
36	Confidence	Ideas friends are usually very important	4	3	2	1
37	Assertive	Opinions from friends are always rights	4	3	2	1
38	Gossip	Friends always gossips about other students	4	3	2	1
39	Irresponsible	'I don't care', I live my life the way I want to	4	3	2	1
40	Sex phobia	Girls like to disturb us a lot	4	3	2	1
41	Social interaction	I usually like to stay alone and keep my thoughts to myself (reversed)	1	2	3	4
42	Aggressiveness	Friends usually threatens to fight me	4	3	2	1
43	Quarrelsome	Friends always quarrels for nothing	4	3	2	1
44	Inquisitive	I do not like getting involve on things that do not concern me	4	3	2	1
45	Unfriendly	Friends usually disturbed my peace	4	3	2	1
46	Uncoopera	Our delegate/leader not	4	3	2	1

	tive	compromising with us				
47	Sullen	They always accused for insulting	4	3	2	1
48	Jovial	Making fun is usually dangerous	4	3	2	1
		Scale D: Emotional Adjustment 9 items				
49	Moody	It is always good to think of pass issues	4	3	2	1
50	Happiness	I am not usually happy in class (reversed)	1	2	3	4
51	Restlessnes s	I feel sometimes uneasy in class	4	3	2	1
52	Hyper-active	I feel good when we have class debate or discussions	4	3	2	1
53	Withdrawn	I like to be left alone	4	3	2	1
54	Stressful	Sometimes is best to think deeply	4	3	2	1
55	Weakness	I usually feels tired or lacks energy	4	3	2	1
56	Temperam ent	Most of the time friends say thinks to annoyed me	4	3	2	1
57	Playful	I loved joking a lot with friends (reversed)	1	2	3	4